# Hello Kitty's

## Book of
# Friendship Fun & Activities

### by Kim Ostrow

**Scholastic Inc.**

New York    Toronto    London    Auckland    Sydney
Mexico City    New Delhi    Hong Kong    Buenos Aires

ISBN 0-439-61918-1

12 11 10 9 8 7 6 5 4 3 2 1          4 5 6 7 8 9/0

Printed in the U.S.A.

First Scholastic printing, January 2004

Book Design by Kay Petronio

# CONTENTS

# Introduction

Ever wanted to throw an amazing birthday party but weren't sure where to begin? Or wondered what kinds of snacks to serve at your next slumber party? Look no further—it's all here, Hello Kitty style!

Hello Kitty loves hanging out with her friends! She and her gal pals love to get together and play games, make cool crafts, eat tasty treats, and lots more. And now Hello Kitty wants to show you how to do all that and more! Learn how to throw the best sleepovers, birthday bashes, outdoor events, and parties away from home. Now you have cool ideas and awesome advice at your fingertips. But that's only the beginning!

Hopefully some of these super suggestions will inspire you to come up with a few party ideas of your own. The only limit is your imagination. Remember there's always one ingredient that will make any party a huge success —great friends!

P.S.—Don't forget about all the supercool STICKERS packed inside. Use them to seal your party envelopes, decorate your invites, make party favors, or just stick them anywhere you want!

# Spa-tacular Sleepover

Hello Kitty says, "Get your friends together for the ultimate beauty experience!"

What better way is there to relax with your friends than spa treatments at a sleepover? Nada. Other than the spa treatments listed in Awesome Activities on page 8, you can find more easy-to-make spa treatments in beauty and fitness magazines. And remember, a spa sleepover is a great way to spend extra time with extra-special friends.

## Inviting Invitation Ideas:

Why not write out the invite just like a recipe? Write the information on index or recipe cards, replacing ingredients with party info. As an added bonus, sprinkle some flower petals in the envelopes—for some sweet-smelling confetti. Don't forget to use the STICKERS, too.

## Designer Decorations:

Drape some fluffy towels over a large table. To add a nice touch, put fresh flowers in water. Or, take a walk outside and collect pretty leaves to scatter around. You can also fill little bowls with smooth stones, seashells, or anything you can find that brings a little nature inside. Place a few lit candles around your room (ask your parents for help), dim the lights, and put on some mellow music for your very own bedroom spa!

## Yummy Snack:

Nothing says healthful like *Fruity Kabobs*!

### Ingredients
- Any fruits
- 1 cup chocolate chips

- Make sure to ask for an adult's help. Chop up your favorite fruits and place them on a bamboo skewer.

- If you're going to serve them at night, make a little chocolate sauce for dipping. All you have to do is put a cup of chocolate chips in a microwave-safe dish and melt on High for 30 seconds, or until smooth.

- If your kabobs are a morning treat, dip them in yogurt.

DELISH!

# Awesome Activities:

Get ready for some super spa treatments that you can do in your own home. Make sure to have enough ingredients, bowls, and mixing spoons for all your guests.

## Oatmeal Face
Put a smile on your face with this simply fabulous facial.

What each guest will need:
- 2 tablespoons oatmeal
- 2 teaspoons honey
- 1 egg white

Mix all together until you have a gooey paste. Apply to your face. Relax for 15 minutes. Giggle at how silly you and your friends look. Rinse with cool water.

## Banana Butterfingers
It's okay to have "butterfingers" after this treatment!

What each guest will need:
- 1/2 ripe banana
- 2 tablespoons butter

Mash banana and butter together until it's nice and smooth. Rub on hands for 10 minutes. Rinse off.

Smooth as a banana peel!

# Cool Craft: Sleeping Bag Sachets

Make some sweet-smelling souvenirs for your friends.

**What you'll need (per guest):**
- A large square of fabric, a bandanna, or a handkerchief
- Fabric glue
- Potpourri
- Ribbon

How to do it:
- Fold material in half.
- Glue two sides together, to form a pouch.
- Fill the pouch with potpourri about halfway.
- Gather at top and tie with ribbon.

Place sachets in your friends' sleeping bags for sweet dreams!

sweet dreams!

# Swapping Spree

Hello Kitty says, "Swapping is a perfect way to share your favorite things with your favorite friends!"

A swap night is a great way to get to know your friends better and to introduce different sets of friends to one another. Everyone will be trading stories and loot all night long. And your friends won't have to go home early because they're sleeping over. Try to keep these parties small—it's easier and way more fun.

## Inviting Invitation Ideas:

Get a notepad and make your invite look like a shopping list! Instruct your guests to bring some of their favorite things, such as an article of clothing, favorite book, CD, etc. Ask your friends to bring photographs of themselves. Don't forget to use the STICKERS, too.

## Designer Decorations:

Decorate your room like a department store by putting fake prices and sale signs on things, have shopping

bags handy, and make a fake display of items. When your guests arrive, place all their items around the store. If you have any paper bags, draw or paint your store logo on them—so your guests can take home their loot in style!

## Yummy Snack:

Since this a swapping party, ask each of your guests to make a favorite party treat to share. If you can't think of anything, how about making some *Sweet Celery Stalks*?

Ingredients:
- Celery stalks
- Peanut butter
- Raisins

- Make sure to ask for an adult's help. Cut the celery stalks into halves.
- Spread on the peanut butter.
- Sprinkle raisins on the celery stalks.
- It's easier than pie and more healthful.

Enjoy!

## Awesome Activity:

### Swap 'n' Share

Everyone should put the items that they brought to the party around the room. Then everyone can "shop" and pick up what other guests brought. Have the owner of the item share with everyone why it's their favorite thing or why it's important to them. Not only will you be swapping stuff, you'll be swapping stories, too.

## Cool Craft:

### Friendly Frames

Remember how you asked each guest to bring in a few photos of themselves? You and your friends can make personalized picture frames for them.

**What you'll need:**
• Popsicle sticks

• Glue

• Decorations of your choice (buttons, paint, markers, sequins, glitter . . .)

How to do it:

- Make a square out of the sticks and glue together. Once they dry, glue another square around the original square.

- Once that dries, pick a side to be the back and glue a stick diagonally from one corner to another. This is what will hold the photo in place.

- Decorate the front of the frame and place the picture in the frame. Then pass it on to one of your friends.

- By the time everyone's finished, you'll have a few framed photos of your gal pals!

# Camp-In

Hello Kitty says, "Now you don't have to wait for the summer to go camping—you don't even have to go outside!"

Camping outside can be fun, but who wants to deal with the bugs, bad weather, and poison ivy? Camping indoors solves all those problems. Plus, you can still tell stories all night, eat goodies like s'mores, and hang with your friends until you fall asleep in your comfy sleeping bag.

## Inviting Invitation Ideas:

Get some dark-colored construction paper and aluminum foil. With a pencil, draw stars on the sheet of foil and cut them out. Glue the stars onto your invitation. Don't forget to use the STICKERS, too.

## Designer Decorations:

If you have a tent to pitch inside, great! If not, just make enough room for all of your friends' sleeping bags.

Decorate the room with cutouts of stars, maybe even stick some glow-in-the-dark stickers on them so when the lights are out, you feel like you're actually outside. To create a campfire, pile a few strings of Christmas lights. Then cover them with red and yellow cellophane. See if you can find some rocks and twigs outside to surround your "campfire."

## Yummy Snack:

### Indoor S'mores

are great once you're done chowing down on dinner!

**Ingredients:**
Graham crackers
Milk chocolate
Marshmallows

- Make sure to ask for an adult's help. Preheat the oven to 300°F.
- Place one half of the cracker on aluminum foil, with marshmallow on top.
- Bake for 4 minutes.
- Remove from oven and immediately place chocolate on top, then the other half of the cracker.
- Chocolate, marshmallows, and crunchy graham crackers—how can you go wrong?

# Awesome Activity:

## Dare to Be Scared

When you and your guest are tucked in, get ready to be spooked. Turn off the lights and go around the room to see who can tell the scariest story. Make sure to place your flashlight directly under your chin while you tell your terrifying tale. Once everyone is good and scared, sing some campfire songs to lighten the mood. You'll never notice that you're not outside!

# Cool Craft:

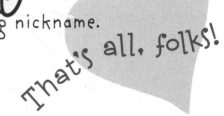

## Flashy Flashlights

These "flashy" gifts are useful and will light up everyone's life—outdoors or under the covers!

What you'll need:
• Flashlights
• Paint pens or paint and paintbrushes
• Glitter

How to do It:
• Have everyone choose a camping nickname.
• Paint it on your flashlight.
• Drop glitter over wet paint.
• Let them dry.

That's all, folks!

## Camping Cushions

Make a cute, comfortable cushion for each of your guests to take home.

**What you'll need:**

- 2 square pieces of patterned fabric or 2 large bandannas
- Iron-on vinyl
- Iron
- Scissors
- Sewing machine and thread
- Straight pins
- Soft filler like an old pillow, stuffing, or foam batting

**How to do it:**

- Make sure to ask for an adult's help. Read the instructions on the iron-on vinyl's package.
- Then, iron the iron-on vinyl to the patterned sides of the square pieces of fabric or large bandannas.
- Pin the two pieces of fabric together with the pattern showing on the outside.
- Sew the two pieces together leaving space on one side open, so you can stuff it with the soft filler.
- Turn the fabric and stuff with the old pillow or stuffing.
- Now your friends can take a seat in the great outdoors or indoors!

# Groovy Movie

Hello Kitty says, "Lights! Camera! Action! Time to party!"

Go to the movies without leaving your house! Plus, you will be able to share your favorite films with your friends. Or each one of your friends can bring a favorite film on video or DVD to watch. The best part is that you do not have to buy a ticket and you can fall asleep during the movie because it's a sleepover!

## Inviting Invitation Ideas:

You can't get into a movie without a ticket. So why not make one as an invitation? Have your guests bring their ticket invitations to the party, then you can tear off half as they walk through the door! Don't forget to use the STICKERS, too.

## Designer Decorations:

What's the best thing about the movies? The concession stand! Set up a goody table where guests can choose junk food and healthy snacks. Also, popcorn bags are cheap and you can fill them with either homemade or store-bought popcorn.

## Yummy Snack:

Instead of regular old pizza, why not some *Cheesy Quesadillas*? This recipe serves 4.

Ingredients:
- 8 flour tortillas
- 2 cups shredded cheese
- 2 cups different chopped vegetables like tomatoes, onions, peppers
- Cooking spray

- Make sure to ask for an adult's help. Preheat oven to 400°F.
- Spray the baking sheet with cooking spray.
- Place one tortilla on a baking sheet, pile on the toppings and cheese, then sandwich it with the other flour tortilla.

- Spray the top tortilla's outside with cooking spray. Bake for 7–10 minutes. Let cool for 2 minutes.
- Then slice into wedges, like pizza!
- Yum, yum, yum!

## Awesome Activity:

### Winner's Choice

Before everyone sits down to watch the movie, why not play a few rounds of charades—using only movie titles? Or to mix things up, you can use your favorite movie stars and Hollywood hotties. Split up into teams. Whichever team wins gets to choose the first movie to watch. Plus, it's a better way to start a movie than watching boring commercials or trailers!

## Cool Craft:

### Superstar Pillowcase

You'll always have sweet dreams with your pretty personalized pillowcase!

What you'll need:
- White pillowcases
- Fabric paints, glitter marker, pens

How to do it:

- Draw a star, like on the Hollywood Walk of Fame, on each pillow.

- Each guest signs her name in the middle.

- You can trace your hands—just like a real movie star. Decorate away.

- Voilà! You and your friends have your own personalized bedtime star!

# Now You're Cooking

Hello Kitty says, "Learning new things makes for lasting memories!"

Cooking for friends can be easy even on your birthday. All you have to do is keep your meal simple. You can start off with something easy like a salad. The main dish could be filling, but easy to make like French Bread Pizzas found in the Yummy Snacks section on the next page. You can top it all off with a fruit salad, yogurt with chopped fruit, or Cupcakes to Bake found on page 24. See—it's not that hard! The best part about cooking for all your friends is that it is a terrific thank-you for visiting.

## Inviting Invitation Ideas:

Get some paper and design a menu. Decide what you're going to cook and decorate the menu accordingly. Don't forget to use the STICKERS, too.

## Designer Decorations:

Decorate your kitchen and dining area like a restaurant. Set the table with white napkins and put some candles or flowers on the table. This is your very own business, so use your imagination to decorate the way you'd like your restaurant to look.

## Yummy Snacks:

*French Bread Pizzas* is an easy treat to make— and eat! This recipe serves 2.

Ingredients:
- French bread
- Tomato sauce
- Grated cheese
- Chopped veggies

- Make sure to ask for an adult's help. Preheat the oven to 425° F.
- Slice bread lengthwise. Place both halves of bread on aluminum foil cover baking pan.
- Slather each with sauce, toppings, then cheese.
- Bake for 15 minutes.
- Soon you and your friends will be munching on pizza! Serve with salad for a balanced meal.

# Cupcakes to Bake

are a sweet, sweet ending to a birthday bash. And before you know it, they'll all be gone!

*Now, you're one cool chef!*

**Ingredients:**
- 2 softened sticks unsalted butter
- 2 cups sugar
- 4 large eggs
- 1 1/2 cups self-rising flour
- 1 1/4 cups all-purpose flour
- 1 cup milk
- 1 teaspoon vanilla extract

- Make sure to ask for an adult's help. Preheat oven to 350° F.
- Mix butter with a mixer on a medium speed or by hand until smooth. Add sugar, and beat until the mixture is fluffy. Then add the eggs and continue to mix.
- Combine the flours and add to batter. Then add the milk and the vanilla. Beat well after you add each ingredient.
- Spoon the batter into two muffin pans lined with cupcake papers. Bake for about 25 minutes, or until you can stick a toothpick in a cupcake and it comes out clean. Then cool and remove cupcakes from pans.
- Make your cupcakes extra delish with a dab of frosting and a toss of sprinkles.

# Awesome Activity:

## Cooking 1-2-3

Teach your friends something new at this party. Choose what you'd like to cook. It should be simple or else you'll drive your friends and parents crazy. Make copies of the recipe for everyone to follow. For example, all your friends can learn to make their own pizza dough. It's easy-to-make, not too messy, and they can freeze it to use later. Make sure to talk with a parent and decide what's doable. Or if making something is too hard or too much work, try decorating desserts instead, like personalizing store-bought cupcakes with icing and sprinkles.

# Cool Craft:

## Amazing Aprons

These great gifts have style & will keep your clothes clean!

What you'll need:
- Inexpensive canvas aprons
- Paint pens or paint and paintbrushes
- Glitter
- Glue

How to do it:
- Give everyone an apron.
- Decorate away—paint, and glue glitter. Just make it fab!
- Let them dry.
- Put them on. It's that easy.

# Crafty Party

Hello Kitty says, "Do-it-yourself parties let you and your friends be as creative as you want to be!"

There's more to a birthday bash than a big cake. Try a do-it-yourself craft party to give your birthday party a twist. The craft to be made during the party can be as simple as a Bead My Friend Bracelet on page 28. Take a trip to your favorite craft or discount store and stock up on bulk items like beads, string, glitter, paper, paint, glue, etc. Decide if you want everyone to paint or bead—or both. The best part of this party is that everyone gets a gift.

## Inviting Invitation Ideas:

Try your hand at gluing a border around the invitation, using any of the craft elements you want at your party. Use beads, glitter, feathers, sequins, or paints—the more, the merrier! Don't forget to use the STICKERS, too.

## Designer Decorations:

Clear off the biggest table in your home. As always, ask permission first. Lay down newspaper to protect the table. Set up different stations for all the crafts you'll offer at your party. Get some inexpensive plastic trays and paint your friends' names on them. This will give everyone a work space—and a fun thing to bring home.

## Yummy Snacks:

In keeping with the do-it-yourself theme, you can make food stations for your guests, too. A salad bar can be lots of fun. Arrange all the add-on ingredients like lettuce, tomatoes, cheese, onions, and dressing in bowls. Then for dessert, arrange an ice cream sundae bar—include bowls of chocolate chips, fruit, nuts, and cookie bits.

Mmmmm—ice cream!

# Awesome Activity:

## Candy Craft

It might also be fun to make edible neck-laces for each guest before they arrive. Use candies that have holes. And then string them together—both stylish and sweet! Give the necklaces out as each of your friends arrives. Now they'll have something to munch on and talk about as the party gets started.

# Cool Crafts

## Bead My Friend Bracelet

Have your friends make beautiful beaded bracelets for themselves or their other friends.

What you'll need:
- 4mm or 6mm beads (gets lots of different colors)
- Elastic stringing cord
- Glue

How to do it:
- Cut a 12" long piece of elastic stringing cord.
- Double knot one end.
- Stiffen the other end of the cord with the glue, so it's easier to string through the beads.

- Select two or more colors of the beads. Then string beads on the elastic cord by alternating colors, so you make a pattern.
- Continue until you have a long enough string to fit around your wrist. Then tie off the open end of the cord with a double knot.
- Tie both ends together, and slip it on your wrist. That's wasn't so hard!

## Tablecloth to Treasure

Here's a chance for your friends to give you something to remember your special day.

What you'll need:
- A big white sheet
- Fabric markers
- Glitter
- Beads  • Glue

How to do it:
- Put the white tablecloth on your craft table where everyone is working.
- As your guests are stringing friendship bracelets, painting pictures, or working on other crafts, have them take a little time to write you a birthday message or draw a picture on your tablecloth.
- They can even glue glitter and beads on it, too.
- When they're done, you'll have a wonderful souvenir to treasure!

# Tea for More than Two

Hello Kitty says, "A tea party is a delightful way to spend the afternoon."

Day or night, there's always time for tea. A tea party is a great way to celebrate your big day elegantly. Sometimes it's a nice change of pace to not have a wild, crazy party—and your parents will thank you, too! Plus it gives you and your friends a reason to get all dressed up. And tasty sweet treats always go with tea.

## Inviting Invitation Ideas:

You can write out your invites on construction paper that's cut into the shapes of teacups. If you're feeling particularly creative, cover each one with pretty scrapbook paper or wrapping paper. You can even glue a lace border on it. Include a lovely teabag inside the envelope for a fancy touch. Don't forget to use the STICKERS, too.

## Designer Decorations:

This party is all about pretty things and elegance. Set the table with flowers and candles. Use the most charming plates you can find—even if they're paper. Make place cards and use your best pens to write out your guests' names.

## Yummy Snacks:

Take this opportunity to introduce your friends to delicious new teas. If it's warm out, make iced tea instead. Serve small pieces of cakes, cookies, fresh fruit, and these *Tiny Tea Sandwiches.*

Ingredients:
- Loaf of sliced white bread
- Cucumber slices
- Cream cheese
- Cookie cutters (any shape you like)

- Spread cream cheese on one slice of bread. Then add the sliced cucumber slices.
- Top it with another slice of bread. Cut off the crusts.
- Use your cookie cutter to create cute shapes.

- You can use other fillings, too. Try peanut butter and banana, tuna salad, or tomato and cheese. Just make sure it tastes good!

In case, some of your pals don't like tea. Have no fear, make some *Gingery Lemonade.* It's sweet and a little bit spicy! This recipe serves 10.

Ingredients:
- 2 quarts water
- 1 1/2 cups white sugar
- 7 slices ginger root
- 2 cups fresh lemon juice

- Make sure to ask for an adult's help. Combine sugar, water, and ginger root in a large pot. Then heat the pot until the water starts boiling. Stir for a few minutes and then remove pot from stove.
- Stir in lemon juice. Remove ginger with a strainer. Then chill lemonade in refrigerator.
- Just pour into glasses and watch your friends drink away and smile.

It's sweet and a little bit spicy!

## Awesome Activity:
### Party Poem

Another thing that adds elegance to a tea party is a poetry reading. Have paper and pens ready. Pick a subject for your tea party poem. Have each guest write a line, cover it, and pass it on. Have the last person read it out loud.

## Cool Craft:
### Jewel Cups

Now you and your gal pals can feel like princesses when you sip tea from this sparkly cup!

**What you'll need:**
- Inexpensive plastic teacups
- Fake gems, jewels, or rhinestones
- Glue gun or fast-drying adhesive (make sure to ask for a parent's help when using either)

**How to do it:**
- Carefully decorate your cup with the jewels. Try to use a consistent pattern around the outside of the cup. Let the cup dry.
- Now drink tea in style! Or you can leave it by your bed and use it to hold your favorite rings or necklaces.
- Just be gentle and be sure to hand wash and not to place in the dishwasher.

33

# Disco Dance Party

Hello Kitty says, "Dance, dance, dance the night away!"

Have a boogie-down birthday with all your friends. The key to this party is music. So get all your favorite CDs and tapes together and hit "Play." Ask your friends to bring their favorite jams to get the party started on the right note. You and your friends will have an awesome time getting your blood pumping as the music moves you!

## Inviting Invitation Ideas:

Cut out construction paper into the shape of a CD, or you can buy a pack of blank CDs and glue your invite to them. As an added touch, you can add pictures of your favorite pop, rock, and hip-hop stars to decorate the invite. Don't forget to use the STICKERS, too.

## Designer Decorations:

Figure out where you have the most space to dance the night away. String up some lights. Try to find a cheap disco ball to hang on the ceiling or something else shiny to be the centerpiece of the dance floor. Set up a DJ area for your stereo. Then all your guests can take turns choosing what to play. It's a groovy way to spend the night!

## Yummy Snack:

Dancing makes everyone hungry—so have lots of treats to keep their energy going. Bowls of chips, nuts, fruit, candy—whatever you think your friends will munch on. When your guests first arrive, they can have some bite-sized *Dancing Dogs* to chow down on.

### Ingredients:

- Hot dogs (or veggie dogs)
- Package of instant crescent roll dough
- Slices of cheese
- Ungreased cookie sheet

- Make sure to ask for an adult's help. Cut the hot dogs into quarters.

- Roll out the dough.
- Slit hot dog pieces and place cheese inside.
- Wrap some dough around each bite-sized piece.
- Put them on the cookie sheet.
- Follow directions on crescent roll package to find out what temperature to preheat oven to and how long to bake.
- Crescent rolls should be golden brown when ready.
- Cool for a few minutes. Then serve.

Eat'em up and then head back onto the dance floor.

## Awesome Activity:

### Dance, Dance, Dance!

There are lots of ways to make this more than a dance party. Have dance contest, but give everyone a prize so no one feels left out. See who can invent the best or worst new dance moves. Or see who can dance for the longest time nonstop. Have your guests be the judges. If you don't feel like dancing all night long, you can rent a dance movie to end the night.

# Cool Craft:

## Disco Mirror

Mirror, mirror on the wall who is the best dancer of them all? You and your friends can ask your disco mirror this question, but not until you make it.

**What you'll need:**
- Inexpensive round mirrors (either compact-sized or larger)
- Silver glitter
- Glue
- Construction paper
- Tape

How to do it:

- Using construction paper, cut out a circle that is slightly smaller than the circumference of your mirror.

- Tape the circle to the mirror—this will protect the mirror from getting glitter all over it and create a template for the glitter.

- Run glue along the perimeter of the exposed mirror. Carefully sprinkle glitter on the glue. Let dry very well. Slowly remove paper.

- Now you can see your disco diva self in this mirror!

Hello Kitty says, "It's always good to mix things up!"

## Inviting Invitation Ideas:

On a piece of your favorite stationery or paper, write the entire invitation info backwards, so your guests have to decode it by looking in a mirror. Remind your friends to wear all their clothes backwards. Don't forget to use the STICKERS, too.

## Designer Decorations:

This party is full of the unexpected, so your room should be as well. Attach balloons and streamers to the floor! If you have a small table, you can set a tablecloth and plates under it. Flip posters, your clock, pictures, and anything else that's not heavy but try not to make a mess!

38

## Yummy Snacks:

Here's a fun idea: Eat the birthday cake first! When you're done, move on to the next course! Put bowls out and fill them with drinks. Put snacks in water glasses! And nothing says backwards like a *Pineapple Upside Down Birthday Cake!*

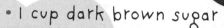

## Ingredients:

- 1/2 cup (1 stick) butter
- 1 cup dark brown sugar
- 1 packet yellow cake mix
- 2 cups sour cream
- 4 large eggs
- 1 16 oz. can of pineapple rings

- Make sure to ask for an adult's help. Preheat oven to 350° F. Place butter in a medium-sized rectangular cake pan and then place pan in oven to melt the butter.

- Mix cake mix, eggs, and sour cream together evenly in a large bowl to make batter. Remove pan from oven and add brown sugar evenly over the melted butter.

- Place pineapple slices in a pattern on top of the butter mixture. Pour batter evenly over the pineapples.

- Bake for 30-40 minutes, or until you can stick a toothpick in it and it comes out clean. Cool for 15 minutes and then flip onto a large plate.

- Serve with whipped cream and/or ice cream as an extra-sweet birthday treat.

# Awesome Activity:

## Goofy Games

Before the party, fill jars with objects like pennies, jelly beans, gumballs, rocks, etc. Remember to count how many objects you put in each jar. Then have each guest guess how many objects are in the jars. Remember, this is a backwards party so whoever's guess is the most off wins—but keep that part a surprise.

Another fun thing to do is have a backwards talent contest. Guests can sing a song backwards or tell a story or joke that starts with the ending first.

# Cool Craft:

## Backwards Bags

Here's a great party favor for your friends. Make inside-out bags for them.

What you'll need:
- Inexpensive canvas totes
- Fabric materials (scraps of old jeans, shirts, bandannas)
- Fabric glue
- Fabric paint

How to do it:

- Cut out square or rectangular shapes from the scrap fabric—as many or as little as you like. These will be the outside pockets of the bag.

- Glue them to the outside of the bag.

- Then, with your fabric paint, write out the name of each of your guests— backwards of course.

- Now your friends have a funky little bag to carry things in and remind them of your birthday.

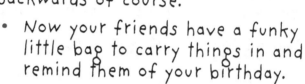

A funky little bag to carry things in!

# Garden Get-Together

Hello Kitty says, "Friends, flowers, and fun make a gorgeous garden party!"

The beauty of a garden party is that you and your closest pals will be enjoying nature. Try to incorporate as much nature into this outing as possible. This is a great reward for you and your friends after a rough week of school. It'll be a natural hit!

## Inviting Invitation Ideas:

Cut out your favorite garden-related shapes—butterflies, flowers, and trees from construction paper. Then write your party info on the shapes. Glue leaves or pressed flowers onto the invite to make it have more nature elements. Don't forget to use the STICKERS, too.

## Designer Decorations:

Spread out some blankets in your backyard so your friends can sit down and relax in the sun. Make sure to space them out a little, so everyone isn't crowded in one

spot. Set up a treats table outside for your party snacks. Ask your parents to help you cut flowers, branches, and leaves, so you can decorate your table with them.

## Yummy Snack:

You and your guests can chill with cold glasses of *Fruity Punch!*

Ingredients:
- 1/2 cup lemon juice
- 1/2 cup sugar
- 2 quarts apple cider
- 2 quarts orange juice
- 2 cups pineapple juice
- 8 whole cloves
- 4 cinnamon sticks (3-4 inches long, each)
- 4 whole oranges sliced up and peeled

- Make sure to ask for an adult's help. Get a large pot. Put all ingredients inside the pot except the orange slices.

- Heat the punch until it boils. Then turn down the heat and let the punch simmer for about 15 minutes.

- Use a large spoon or small strainer to remove the

cloves and cinnamon sticks out of the punch. You can throw the used cloves and cinnamon sticks away.

- Pour the punch from the pot into your punch bowl or container. Then, drop in the orange slices.
- Chill your punch in the refrigerator for a couple of hours before the party.
- Now you and your friends can sit back, relax, and sip some sweet, sweet punch.

## Awesome Activity:
### Quiet Time

A garden party is about relaxing and enjoying nature. Quiet activities are the way to go. Bring out your favorite board games to play. Read passages from your favorite book to your guests. You can always play charades if you and your guests want to do something a little more active.

# Cool Craft:
## Lovely Ladybugs

Ladybugs are not only a great helper in the garden, but also a wonderful inspiration for a crafty souvenir for your guests.

**What you'll need:**
- Small smooth oval rocks
- Large piece of black felt
- Black, red, & white acrylic paint
- White glue
- Spray varnish
- Scissors

How to do it:

- Clean rocks. Then dry them.
- Paint each rock with red paint. Then let each one dry completely.
- Paint a head, a stripe down the back, and spots with black paint.
- Paint the two eyes with white paint.
- After the paint has completely dried, spray each rock with varnish.
- From the black felt, cut out an oval base for each rock. Glue base to the bottom of the ladybug.
- Now, your friends will have a ladybug that they can take inside their homes.

# Everything's Beach-y

Hello Kitty says, "Bring the beach to your backyard!"

Though there's nothing like the beach, sometimes it's too much of a hassle getting there because it's too far away, your parents can't give you a ride, the beach isn't open, etc. With a little creativity and hard work, you can transform your backyard into a small sandy getaway for you and your friends!

## Inviting Invitation Ideas:

Buy a few beach balls from a toy store. Write out the party info with paint pens or glitter paint. Your guests will have to inflate the beach balls to get the 411 on your party. Remind your guests to bring a bathing suit and sunblock! Don't forget to use the STICKERS, too.

## Designer Decorations:

Go to your local hardware store with your parents and get a couple of bags of sand to make a little beach-front. Make sure to lay down enough large garbage bags and then pour sand on them to make your backyard beach. This will make it easier for you to remove the sand after the party. Of course, you'll need a water element for cooling down. If you don't have a pool, then sprinklers are a great substitute and just as much fun!

## Yummy Snack:

Nothing's cooler at a hot beach party than serving *Way Cool Watermelon Ices!* This recipe serves 8.

### Ingredients:

- 8 cups cubed and seeded watermelon (no rind)
- 1 cup water
- 2/3 cup sugar
- 1/4 cup lime juice
- 1 cup chocolate chips

- Make sure to ask for an adult's help. Mix sugar and water in a small saucepan. Bring to a boil and cook until sugar is dissolved. Then let cool.

- Puree the watermelon in a blender. Then combine with sugar syrup and lime juice in a bowl.

- Now pour the mixture into a large rectangular baking dish. Put dish in freezer for 2 hours.
- Scoop mixture into a blender. Then blend until mixture is smooth, but still icy.
- Serve in ice cream dishes and drop some chocolate chips on top. TASTY!

## Awesome Activities:

### Fun in the Sun

Have a game of Limbo. Use a garden hose instead of a broom for people to try to Limbo under. It might be cool to have a water balloon toss. Team up into pairs. Throw a balloon filled with water back and forth and take a step further back with each catch. Can you guess what happens when someone doesn't catch the water balloon—SPLASH!

Don't forget to tell everyone to apply sunscreen when they're out in the sun. There's nothing fun about sunburns!

# Cool Craft:

## *Ocean Bottle*

Your guests can create their own little ocean, bottle it up, and take it home with them.

**How to do it:**

- Pour sand into a bottle until it is half full.

- Then pour a tablespoon of glitter in.

- Next drop in a few seashells, plastic fish, and other ocean objects to personalize your bottle of sea.

- Tint a large container of water blue with food coloring. Pour bluish water into the bottle until it's almost full.

- Put some glue into the lid of the bottle and screw it on to seal the bottle. Let it dry.

- Tip the bottle back and forth to make the ocean move. Don't get seasick!

**What each guest will need:**

- Clean empty plastic soda bottle

- Sand

- Glitter

- Small seashells

- Small plastic fish, seahorses and other ocean objects

- Bottle of blue food coloring

- Water

- Glue

49

# Mystery Time

Hello Kitty says, "There's no mystery as to how to throw a great party—just make it a mystery party!"

## Inviting Invitation Ideas:

Get some manila file folders. Write your friends' names and the phrase "TOP SECRET" across the top of each. Type the party information on a sheet of paper. Ask your guests to dress up as secret agents, undercover officers, detectives, etc. Don't forget to use  STICKERS, too.

## Designer Decorations:

First, get some yellow tape or yellow streamers. Then, in black marker, write "Do Not Cross" on the tape. Now, you have your very own crime scene tape. Place it all over your backyard. Decorate your yard as the scene of the crime.

## Yummy Snack:

You can solve the case of your guests' grumbling stomachs by making some *Disappearing Nachos*!

This recipe serves 4.

**Ingredients:**

- 16 oz. tortilla chips
- 1 cup cheddar cheese, shredded
- 1 cup Monterey Jack cheese, shredded
- 1/2 cup cooked black beans
- 3 finely chopped scallions
- 1 cup diced tomatoes
- 1/2 cup sour cream

- Make sure to ask for an adult's help. Preheat the oven to 400° F. Place the chips in a single layer on a baking pan covered with a baking sheet.

- In a bowl, mix the beans, scallions, and the diced tomatoes. With a spoon, layer the mixture on top of the chips.

- Sprinkle with both cheeses. Bake for 10 minutes or until cheese melts. Then remove from oven.

- Drop some sour cream on top of the nachos and serve.

- Now watch those nachos disappear!

# Awesome Activity:
## Unsolved Mystery

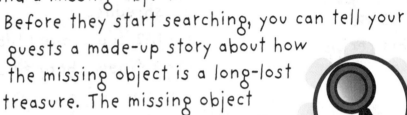

A great mystery for your guests to solve is for them to find a missing object.

Before they start searching, you can tell your guests a made-up story about how the missing object is a long-lost treasure. The missing object clues should lead your guests all around your yard. Type up a clue sheet for each of your friends.

Before the party starts, hide little inexpensive toys and trinkets around your yard like tiny plastic magnifying glasses, fake mustaches, temporary tattoos, etc. This way, all your friends will get a few gifts as they try to find the missing object. The most important thing is to be creative.

# Cool Craft:

## Secret Spy Photo I.D.

Have your guests make their very own all-access I.D. to your party.

**What each guest will need:**
- A wallet-sized photo
- Paper
- Transparent contact paper
- Hole punch
- String or chain
- Marker or glitter pens

How to do it:
- Have everyone choose a detective name.
- On a small square of paper, write out the name along with some made-up, wacky information. Glue photo in the bottom right corner.
- Cover both sides with the contact paper.
- Punch hole in top. Loop in chain or string.
- Place around neck. There you have it!

# fun fund-raising Party

Hello Kitty says, "Spend the day helping others!"

## Inviting Invitation Ideas:

Let your guests know on the invitation that this is a fund-raising party for a charity, such as a children's hospital or animal shelter. Type up a page about the charity you'd like to help and stick it in the envelope. Mention in the invite that you want to raise money by having a car wash, bake sale, running a lemonade stand, etc. Ask your parents for fund-raising ideas. Don't forget to use the STICKERS, too.

## Designer Decorations:

How about making a festive fund-raising headquarters? Make a chart like you see on telethons. Put your goal amount at the top. Use some tape to hang the chart on the wall. You can also hang balloons, smiley faces, and streamers—your fund-raising party doesn't have to be all business!

## Yummy Snack:

It's easy to raise cash with sweet treats, so why not make cookies, cakes, cupcakes, and some *Bake Sale Brownies*? Even if you don't have a bake sale, your friends will need something to munch on while they're fund-raising!

**Ingredients:**
- 4 unsweetened chocolate squares
- 1 cup butter
- 1 cup flour
- 1/4 teaspoon salt
- 4 eggs
- 2 cups sugar
- 2 teaspoons vanilla
- 1 cup chocolate chips

- Make sure to ask for an adult's help. Preheat oven to 350° F. Grease 9 x 13 baking pan.
- Melt chocolate and butter in a large saucepan over low heat. Then let cool.
- In a large bowl, beat eggs until fluffy. Add sugar and beat until thick. Then stir in flour and salt until well blended.
- Blend in chocolate mixture and vanilla. Then stir in the chocolate chips.
- Now, pour brownie batter into greased baking pan.

Bake for 30 minutes or until you can stick a toothpick in it and it comes out clean.

- Let the pan cool then cut brownies into squares.
- Now put out the brownies for your bake sale, or your friends can put them in their mouths—or both!

# Awesome Activities

## Some Bright Ideas

There are many ways to raise money. Make sure to check with your parents before you decide to do any fund-raising. Having a car wash is always a money maker. You and your friends can have fun, raise money, and be on the road to cleaning in no time!

Make sure to put up signs in your neighborhood, so people know that you and your friends are raising money for a charity. Remember to take breaks, play games, goof around, and have a little fun or else everyone will get tired really quickly.

# Cool Craft:
## Extra-Large Card

Once your fund-raising party is over, why not make a huge oversized card for your charity? Create one out of pieces of poster board, markers, paints, tape, glitter, glue, and anything else you and your friends want to decorate it with. Have everyone write a personalized message and sign it. If you have an instant camera

handy, take some pictures of everyone who participated, then paste the pictures to the card. Don't forget to attach an envelope with the money you raised.

# Backyard Olympics

Hello Kitty says, "Be a champ, and go for the gold!"

## Inviting Invitation Ideas:

Cut out construction paper to look like a medal. Glue shiny paper or aluminum foil to the front of it. Type up your party's info on a small piece of paper and attach it to the back of the medal. Don't forget to mention on the invite that guests should dress comfortably and wear sneakers.

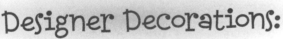

## Designer Decorations:

Choose a few countries and research what their flags look like. Then draw them on construction paper and hang them around your backyard. You'll also need a refreshments table that's off to the side and not in the way of competitions, so athletes/guests can fuel up and get back to the games. You can designate different sporting event areas with banners hung on trees.

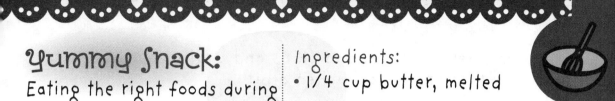

## Yummy Snack:

Eating the right foods during competitions will keep everyone nice and healthy. Make sure to whip up a batch of ***Energy Bars***. They're packed with power! This recipe makes at least 12 servings.

### Ingredients:

- 1/4 cup butter, melted
- 4 large eggs
- 1 cup flour
- 1/2 teaspoon baking powder
- 1/2 cup nonfat milk powder
- 3/4 cup rolled oats
- 1 teaspoon salt
- 1 3/4 cup sugar
- 1 cup raisins
- 1 cup dried cranberries or other dried fruit
- 2 1/2 cups walnuts
- 1 cup chocolate chips

- Make sure to ask for an adult's help. Preheat oven to 350° F. Grease a large baking pan.
- Beat eggs and melted butter together. Then stir in baking powder, milk powder, salt, and sugar.
- Next add flour to egg mixture. Then add raisins, dried

cranberries, nuts, and chips and continue to stir until mixture starts to thicken a bit.

- Spoon mixture into greased baking pan. Spread energy bar mix evenly over pan. Bake for 35 minutes.

- Let pan cool. Then cut into rectangular pieces, wrap the bars in plastic wrap, and freeze.

- Watch as your guests crunch and munch on these tasty healthful treats to satisfy their growling tummies!

# Awesome Activities:
## Let the Games Begin!

This is the heart of your party. Choose fun games that you and your friends will enjoy playing, like jump rope contests, a game of touch football, soccer, tug-o-war, potato sack races, long jumps, relay races, etc.

Also, pick silly and wacky events for your friends to compete in. See who can talk the longest about a subject without stopping to take a breath, get the most apples while bobbing blindfolded, run the fastest through

an obstacle course while singing, or spell the most words backwards correctly, etc.

# Cool Craft:
## *Slammin' Sports T's*

Making these t-shirts is a great way for everyone to take a little break and catch their breath.

What each guest will need:
- 1 inexpensive white T-shirt
- Fabric pens, paintbrushes, and paint
- Glue
- Glitter
- Iron-on sports patches

How to do it:
- Everyone should write their name and their favorite lucky number on the back of their T-shirt with the paint and paintbrushes, fabric pens, or glue and glitter.
- Then decorate the rest of the T-shirt with sports designs and pictures.
- Let the T-shirts dry.
- Make sure to ask for an adult's help. Have your friends iron a patch onto their T-shirts.
- Now, put on that new T-shirt and go out and have some fun with your friends!

# Destination Parties

Sometimes you need to get away from home to throw a great party. Try out these tips for having parties away from home. Keep these parties on the small side, or your parents are going to go crazy and be totally annoyed.

One of the most important things to do is to be organized, so the party planning isn't totally out-of-control. Make sure to make lists and ask for your friends' and parents' opinions before planning anything.

## Location, Location, Location

### Places to Go

Remember to give yourself a little time in advance to decide where you want to go. Thumb through your local paper. There are a lot of great things going on in your community. Get creative. Here are a few suggestions:

- Fireworks shows
- Garden or flower shows
- Free outdoor concerts
- Your favorite author reading at a bookstore or library
- Walking tours
- County fairs
- Park (a full day of scavenger hunts or nature walks)

You can also have parties at places where you have to pay. Call to see how much they charge for everything. If everyone can afford to go and your parents think it's okay, then you're good to go—yay for you! Here are a few places that might be affordable:

- Bowling alleys
- Amusement/water parks
- Farms that let you pick your own fruit

- Movie theater
- Miniature golf
- Carnivals
- The zoo

# What to Bring/Make:
## Snack Packs!

What makes a party even more fun? Food! Spend some time planning snack bags. Get some brown paper lunch bags, decorate them with each of your guests' names, and fill with delicious treats. Sandwiches are always an easy option—along with fruit, cookies, cakes, brownies, cupcakes, or other treats. This book is packed with recipes for tons of tasty treats in the Yummy Snack sections, and a lot of them are easy to pack. Remember, if you're not bringing a cooler, make sure to pack foods that don't need refrigeration.

## Info-Invitations:

For your invitations, be sure to give as much information as possible, like when, where, directions to the place, how much money to bring, what kinds of clothes to wear, what time it will end, what time everyone needs to be picked up, etc.

Decide if you'll meet at your house and go together, or meet at the destination. If you invite a lot of people, make sure enough chaperones can come to supervise. If your party destination is outdoors, think of alternatives in case it rains.

Most importantly, have fun! A destination party may take a little more thought, work, and planning, but your friends are worth it! Plus, it's a great way to show your parents that you're becoming more responsible and mature.